Life in the time of Jesus

Michael Keene

Oliver & Boyd

ACKNOWLEDGEMENTS

The publishers wish to thank the following for permission to reproduce
photographs on the pages listed:
Bible Lands Society (1 top);
Robert Harding (1 bottom, 10, 71 top);
Christine Osborne (8,26 bottom, 43 bottom, 50 bottom, 70,74,78 top right);
Mansell (14 top and bottom, 77);
Sonia Halliday (15,26 top, 27,29 top left, 33,71 bottom left and right, 78 top left and
bottom);
Popperfoto (26 middle left and right, 53);
ZEFA (29 top right and bottom, 30,43 top, 50 top, 64);
National Council of Tourism in Lebanon (38 top);
Camera Press (48 W. Braun and D. Harris);
Hutchison Library (56,69);
Shell (62);
Kinory (66).

Artwork by Bob Geary, Hannah Berridge and Trevor Parkin
Cover illustration by Bob Geary

Oliver & Boyd
Longman House,
Burnt Mill,
Harlow, Essex, CM20 2JE
An Imprint of Longman Group UK Ltd

ISBN 0 05 003972 5

First published 1987
Fifth impression 1992

Produced by Longman Singapore Publishers Pte Ltd
Printed in Singapore

The Publisher's policy is to use paper manufactured from
sustainable forests.

CONTENTS

Introduction

Introduction

Almost two thousand years ago, Jesus was born in a small Middle Eastern country about the same size as Wales. The country was called Palestine and was ruled by the Romans. To the people who lived there, though, who were Jewish, it was known as Israel.

These two pictures are of a village and a town in Israel today. The buildings may have looked something like this two thousand years ago, but life in them was very different.

To understand more about what Jesus said and did we must know something about the country where he was born, and the people's lives. How did they live? What were their laws and who made those laws? What was their religion? How did they earn their living? Did the children go to school? This book will answer some of these questions.

1. THE LAND OF PALESTINE

Geography

The land where Jesus was born was a very small country. From north to south Palestine was less than 270 kilometres long. The tip of the Dead Sea, in the south-eastern corner of the country, is only 80 kilometres from the nearest coast.

The Jordan Valley, running down the middle of the country, cuts out a very deep trench. To the north of this valley the mountains rise impressively and steeply. The peaks of Mount Hermon, for instance, are about 3000 metres above sea-level. It was the summit of this mountain, snow-capped for much of the year, which was clearly visible from the dusty streets of Palestine's capital city of Jerusalem.

Rising in the foothills of Mount Hermon, the River Jordan soon reaches the large Sea (or Lake) of Galilee. On its journey from there to the Dead Sea the river falls sharply as it winds and twists like a snake. The Dead Sea itself is almost 400 metres below sea-level and is the lowest point on earth.

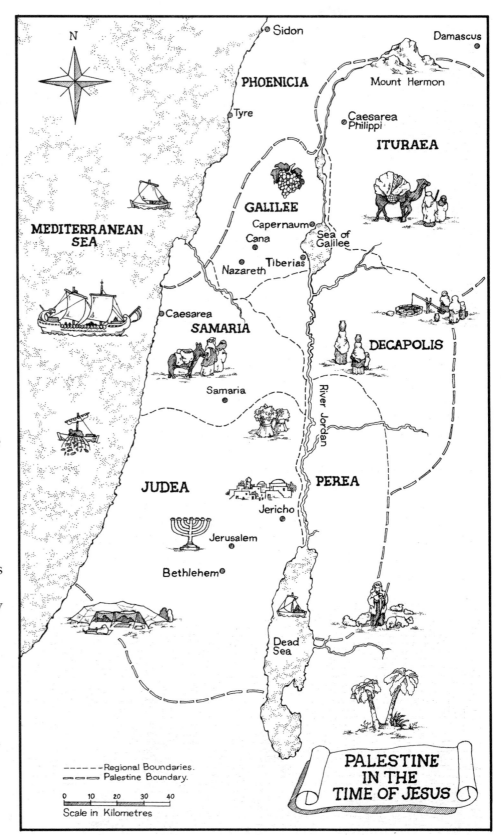

PALESTINE IN THE TIME OF JESUS

------ Regional Boundaries.
-- ◻ -- Palestine Boundary.

0 10 20 30 40

Scale in Kilometres

Climate

Just as the geography of Palestine varied greatly from place to place so did its climate. The climate was mainly a combination of hot and dry summers with mild and wet winters. There was little, if any, rain between June and September. In the deep Jordan Valley the temperature stayed at a steady 37 °C for these four months, although elsewhere it settled at around 26 °C.

In the higher parts of Palestine there were heavy morning dews. These conditions were ideal for growing grapes, cucumbers and melons.

In the winter, snow in Jerusalem and freezing rain elsewhere were fairly common. For most of the time, however, the winters were quite mild.

The amount of rain that fell varied considerably from year to year. Even within such a small country some places were much drier than others.

In Palestine it began to rain each year in October. The rainfall was at its heaviest in December and January before it began to lighten in April. There was then no rain until the following October.

Matthew 7:26, 27; 16:2, 3.

Natural resources

Water

The most important natural resource in Palestine in Jesus's time was water. Apart from the River Jordan most of the streams and rivers in the country were dry for the greater part of the year. People built their towns and villages carefully, near wells or springs.

Reservoirs were built outside large towns to store water and, during the Roman occupation of Palestine, aqueducts were constructed to carry water.

Matthew 10:42; John: 4.

Minerals

There were large natural supplies of copper and iron in the country. Copper was mined from the desert area around the Dead Sea whilst objects made from iron had been used for centuries.

Copper was the most common metal in Palestine. It was melted down in clay pots over a fire and then shaped.

Iron was used to make weapons as well as common everyday items.

Gold, silver and tin were brought in from countries as far away as Britain, Spain and India.

The Sea of Galilee and the River Jordan

The name 'Jordan' gives us a clue to the character of the River Jordan. It means 'the river that rushes down', and that is exactly what it does between Mount Hermon and the Sea of Galilee. After leaving the mountains, the river drops 250 metres in height over a distance of less than 20 kilometres.

The Sea of Galilee is a fresh-water lake. In the time of Jesus it was the main area for fishing in Palestine. Fourteen different species of fish are said to have been found there.

The Sea of Galilee was well known for its sudden squalls and storms. These were caused by the winds being funnelled down the steep sides of the Jordan valley.

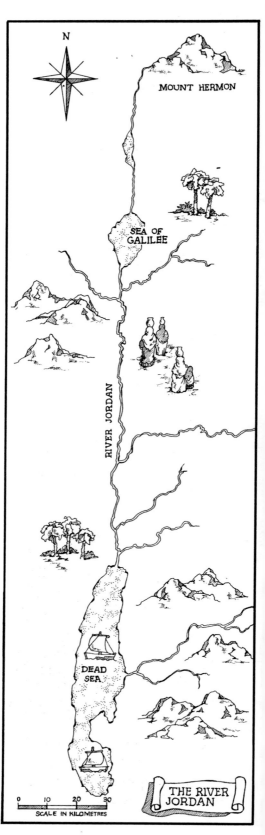

At the southern end of the Sea of Galilee, the River Jordan cuts a deep, winding valley. The river was very difficult to cross at this point.

The third highest temperature ever recorded on earth, 53.8 °C, was recorded in the Jordan Valley in 1929. The summer temperatures in the valley were so high that few people travelled through the area.

Matthew 2:2; 27:55; Luke 3:3.

The Dead Sea

The Dead Sea, the lowest body of water on the earth's surface, is almost 400 metres below sea-level. Situated at the southern end of the country it is 80 km long and only 18 km at its widest point. Because the Dead Sea does not have any outlets it fills with salts and other minerals that are swept down by the fast-flowing River Jordan. As a result the salt content of the water is as high as 25 per cent, five times greater than that found in any ocean.

Fish could only last in its waters a matter of a few minutes. They were often to be seen floating dead on its surface.

No form of green vegetation was able to grow on its banks. The edges of the Dead Sea were totally barren.

The water evaporated in the high temperatures very rapidly. At certain times in the year the Dead Sea almost dried up.

There were vast deposits of salt on its banks and this was sold to people to preserve and season their food.

People can remain afloat in its waters for a long time, although they come out covered in a film of salt!

In Jesus's time, few people wanted to live on its barren and inhospitable shores. Those who did so were mainly nomads (wanderers).

Matthew 5:13.

The city of Jerusalem

Jerusalem lay between two valleys and was divided down the middle by a third. In Jesus's day an aqueduct ran across this valley joining the west side of the city, where Herod had his palace, with the east where the Temple stood. Jerusalem was very crowded. Fifty thousand people lived inside the city walls.

The streets were narrow, steep and unsuitable for wheeled traffic. Camels, mules, donkeys and horses were the main means of transport although most people found it easier to walk. On every street-corner there were traders and travellers. The streets of Jerusalem were always alive with people and during a religious festival it was almost impossible to move.

Shielded by the Judean hills nearby and fanned by a cool breeze blowing off the Mediterranean Sea, the temperature in Jerusalem was lower than almost anywhere else in the country. The annual rainfall, some 66 cm, fell almost totally between November and April.

At the time of Jesus the city of Jerusalem, already at least five thousand years old, was a natural fortress, standing about 900 metres above sea-level. It was almost totally surrounded by deep ravines. Over the centuries, however, these ravines have been filled in, as the photograph of present-day Jerusalem shows.

Luke 13:33–35; 19:28, 37.

Jerusalem today

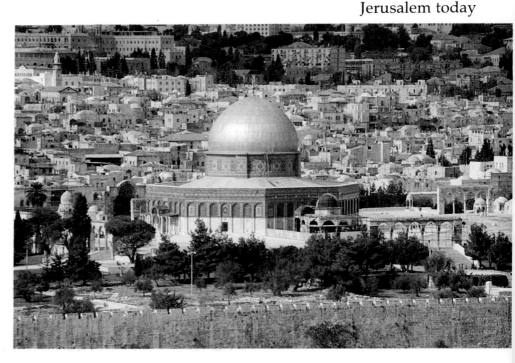

10

Things to do

1. Answer these questions in your own words.
   a) What were the names of the large inland seas in Palestine?
   b) Which river bent and twisted like a snake?
   c) Which was the lowest point on earth?
   d) Which fruit and vegetables grew in Palestine?
   e) How did the people of Palestine make sure that they had enough water?
   f) Which minerals were mined in Palestine and which had to be imported from other countries?
   g) Why was the Dead Sea so 'dead'?

2. Imagine that you had lived in Palestine two thousand years ago. Write a letter to a friend who had never visited the country describing just what it was like to live there. Point out both the advantages and the disadvantages of life.

3. Copy or trace this blank map of Palestine into your books. The important geographical features and towns are listed in the box below. Mark them carefully on your map.

> Sea of Galilee   River Jordan   Dead Sea   Mediterranean Sea
> Jerusalem   Nazareth   Bethlehem   Jericho

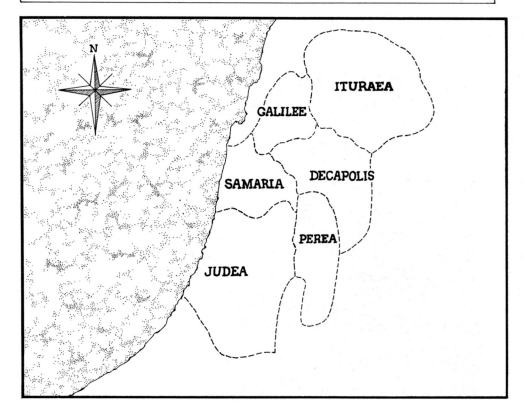

2. PALESTINE UNDER ROMAN OCCUPATION

The Romans move in

The Roman Republic was formed in 509 BC. In its early years the Roman Army was untrained and small but it soon became a well-trained fighting force. The Carthaginian general Hannibal offered a brief threat to Roman power, but he was finally defeated in 202 BC. Then victory over the Macedonians brought the Romans great spoil and treasure, together with thousands of slaves. For some years following this the Romans fought amongst themselves until Julius Caesar emerged as the Empire's undisputed leader.

In 63 BC the Roman General, Pompey, entered Palestine and captured Jerusalem. The period of occupation had begun and the country was not to be free from Roman rule for many years to come.

With its new weapons and tight discipline the Roman Army was the most powerful yet known.

To expand their Empire the Romans:

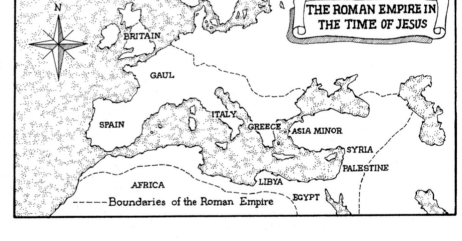

THE ROMAN EMPIRE IN THE TIME OF JESUS

N

BRITAIN

GAUL

SPAIN

ITALY

GREECE

ASIA MINOR

SYRIA

PALESTINE

AFRICA

LIBYA

EGYPT

-----Boundaries of the Roman Empire

made treaties of friendship,

slaughtered their enemies,

robbed cities and villages,

copied the Greek way of life.

The Roman occupation was a great blow to the pride of the people of Palestine. The Romans were destroying their sacred places, breaking their religious laws and imposing very heavy taxes upon them. Athletic Games were held every four years in honour of the Roman Emperor. This offended the Jews as the competitors took part naked.

The Romans left the Jews in no doubt that their country had been occupied. A Roman Governor, Pontius Pilate, ruled in Jerusalem, and Roman soldiers were to be seen everywhere in the city streets. Jewish men, however, were not compelled to serve in the Roman Army.

Although the Romans put down any sign of rebellion ruthlessly they did, on one occasion, give in to the Jews. A Roman soldier threw a sacred Jewish scroll on a fire. The Jews were so annoyed at this outrage that the soldier was put to death on the orders of the Emperor.

There were some benefits to the Jews from the Roman occupation. Trade flourished as good roads were built. Many wealthy Jews copied the Roman style of building.

Mark 15:1,2; Luke 3:1; 13:1.

The Emperors

Augustus — Roman Emperor from 27 BC to AD 14

In 27 BC, Octavian, the son of Julius Caesar, won the support of the Roman people. He came to be called 'Augustus' meaning 'Majesty'. Augustus was the Roman Emperor when Jesus was born. He was a good ruler, who brought a period of real peace to the Roman Empire. He made it possible for people to move freely and safely by land and sea from one part of the Empire to another.

For many years during the reign of Augustus the Army was not on active service.

Augustus conducted a census throughout the Empire. This told the Government how many people should pay taxes.

Tiberius — Roman Emperor from AD 14 to AD 37

Although a good soldier, Tiberius was a cruel tyrant. There were several unsuccessful rebellions in his time.

Towards the end of his life Tiberius was 'retired' to the isle of Capri, where he ended his days in drunkeness.

Luke 2:1, 3:1.

Herod the Great

Herod the Great was ruler in Palestine under the Romans when Jesus was born. The Romans appointed him to rule over the Jews because he was partly Jewish himself. During his lifetime Herod had ten wives and a large number of children. Many of them were put to death by his own orders. Every Jewish man and woman breathed a huge sigh of relief when this cruel King died.

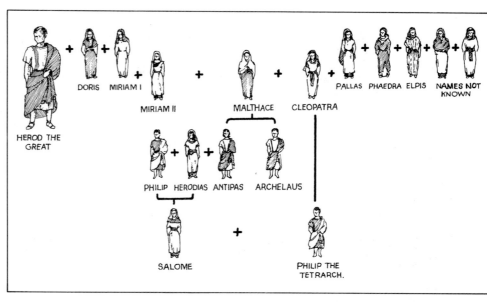

This is part of the family-tree of King Herod.

Amongst Herod's many magnificent buildings was the Temple in Jerusalem (see page 36). He started to build it in 19 BC and it was finally destroyed in AD 70.

When Herod heard that Jesus, the 'King of the Jews', had been born he ordered his soldiers to kill all Jewish boys under the age of two.

Because of his fear of being attacked Herod built many fortresses during his life-time. The most impressive was on the top of a huge outcrop of rock at Masada.

Matthew 2:13–18; Mark 6:14–29; Luke 3:19,20.

Collecting the taxes

People in the countries Rome conquered had to support the Roman Army and pay for the running of the Empire. People in Palestine had to pay taxes in five ways to the Roman authorities:

The Romans collected a toll on all main roads.

One quarter of the value of produce grown on the land had to be paid to the Romans in money or goods.

Censuses were held every five years to decide how much wealth each man had. He was then taxed on that value.

Whenever slaves, farm produce and other goods were sold in the market a 'sales tax' was collected.

Dues were collected at harbours and frontier posts. They were charged on both imports and exports. Although most goods were taxed at a straightforward 2 per cent, certain luxury items, such as perfumes, carried a tax of 25 per cent.

The Romans did not like collecting the taxes themselves as it made them very unpopular with the people. Every five years the right to collect the taxes was auctioned in Rome. The people who bought the right to make the collection made their profit by charging everyone extra. They then hired 'publicans' to do the actual collecting. The publicans also made a profit by charging the people more. No wonder the people felt hard done by!

Matthew 22:17; Luke 18:10; 19.2.

16

Roman roads

Most of the roads in Palestine were very poor and made travelling difficult and dangerous. Few of the ordinary highways were paved. The main roads, however, which the Romans had built, were as straight as possible and very well constructed. They were

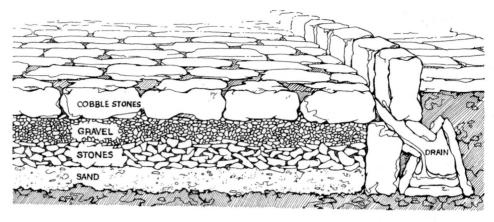

made so that Roman soldiers could travel quickly. When building a road the Romans laid a foundation of sand, stones, gravel and concrete. On top of this was a layer of cobble-stones in mortar. There were drains at the sides to take away rain water.

If you had travelled along a Roman road in Palestine you might have seen:

Roman soldiers on the march; travellers, herds of animals and wagons moving from one town to another; people travelling on foot, by donkey, horse or mule (only the wealthy travelled in a carriage).

Messengers carried the instructions of the Emperor. A courier could cover 200 km in one day with fresh horses.

Many travellers preferred to set up their own tents by the roadside.

Friends might be seen greeting one another as travellers were welcomed after a long journey.

Luke 10:25–37.

The Roman Army

Life was busy for a Roman soldier. Normally there were three thousand Roman soldiers (a legion) stationed in Palestine. A legate was responsible for the control of each legion and the legion was then sub-divided into ten cohorts commanded by a tribune. The cohort was broken down still further into centuries for which a centurion was the responsible officer.

The Roman soldier was the most carefully selected, trained and disciplined of any in the Ancient World. His training included individual and group combat. He was kept in top physical condition by route-marches and exercises. His diet was carefully controlled whilst particular care was taken over the water-supply since this was often a source of infection and disease.

The centurion, on the left below, was chosen from amongst the older Roman soldiers. They were paid about fifteen times as much as the ordinary legionary, below right.

HELMET

SWORD

STAFF

The centurion

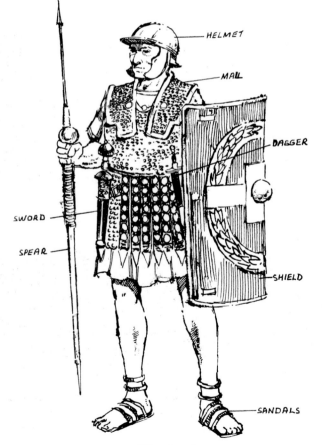

HELMET

MAIL

DAGGER

SWORD

SPEAR

SHIELD

SANDALS

The legionary

Six hundred soldiers were kept in the capital city of Jerusalem. Their biggest problem was to control the large number of people who flooded into the city for the religious festivals.

Roman units were detailed to watch the passage of caravans through Palestine from Egypt, Saudi Arabia and Syria. The soldiers collected taxes from them.

Although slave labour was used by the Romans to build their roads, much of the work was done by soldiers. After the road was completed the soldiers then had the responsibility of policing it.

Roman carriages were expected to travel 40 km in a day. Each team of horses could only manage a third of that distance, so overnight stopping places and posts for changing the horses were established by soldiers.

Matthew 8:5; Luke 3:14.

Crime and punishment

Crucifixion was the Roman penalty for murder, piracy, banditry and rebellion. One Roman Emperor is said to have crucified five hundred men in one day. (He would have crucified more but ran out of wood!) Crucifixion was a very long, slow form of death. Soldiers would break the criminals' legs after a time. As this meant that the victims could not breathe properly, death soon followed.

A criminal was beaten or flogged with thirty-nine strokes. This was forty strokes minus one — in case a mistake had been made in the counting. The whip (or scourge) was made of two or three leather thongs with pieces of bone or metal embedded in them.

Stoning to death was a punishment usually reserved for women – often for committing adultery. Men and women stood around the top of a pit and hurled boulders down on their unfortunate victims until they were dead.

Children were always expected to be obedient to their parents. A son who attacked his father was garrotted, or strangled. An iron collar was put around his neck and tightened.

Luke 10:30; John 19:1; 17—27.

Things to do

1. Here are some words mentioned in this chapter. Explain, in your own words, what they mean.
   a) the title 'Augustus'.   **b)** Publican.
   c) A legion.   **d)** A centurion.   **e)** A tribune.

2. Explain how the Romans raised money by taxing the people who lived in Palestine. If you had lived there which tax would you have considered to have been the most unfair? Why did the Romans employ other people to collect the taxes?

3. Imagine that you were a Roman soldier posted to a garrison in Palestine. Describe what you think your posting would have been like and some of the problems that you might have been called upon to face.

4. Write an essay with the title 'The power of Rome'. In it try to explain why the Roman Empire was so powerful two thousand years ago.

5. On this page is a drawing of a Roman soldier fully equipped for battle. Copy it into your books and label the items listed in the box below the drawing.

| Roman mail | bronze scale armour | shield |
| helmet | dagger | sandals | sword | spear |

3. THE RELIGION OF THE JEWS

The rabbis

In the time of Jesus the rabbis taught the Holy Scriptures to the people. As their work was unpaid most rabbis did another job as well. They also spent a lot of time talking together about the Jewish faith. On one famous occasion they spent hours wondering whether a Jew should eat an egg laid by a chicken on the Sabbath day!

To be a rabbi was to have a life-time in which to study the holy Jewish Scriptures. This was a great honour and privilege.

Every Sabbath day the rabbi was to be found preaching a sermon in the synagogue during the service.

Each rabbi was expected to set an example, for instance, by being generous to the poor. There were beggars in every town.

It was the rabbi's duty to remind people about the special laws concerning their religion, for instance, the ceremonial washing before prayers.

They also reminded people about the kinds of food they could eat (*kosher* food) and the special ways in which it had to be prepared. (See page 44.) Food which was not prepared according to the law (i.e. was not *kosher*) could not be eaten.

Matthew 23:7,8; John 1:38; 6:25.

The Pharisees

The name 'Pharisee' meant the 'separated one' and this gives us a clue as to how the Pharisees lived in Palestine. The Pharisees tried to live holy and separate lives. They did not cooperate with the Romans any more than they could help.

Most of the Pharisees were scribes by profession. These were the people who arranged and copied the Holy Scriptures. As they were considered to be experts, the people went to them for advice when they needed to know what the Scriptures said about any particular problem. This made the people dependent upon them for religious guidance so the Pharisees were a very powerful group of people.

The Pharisees lived strictly by the Law of Moses as it was found in the first five books of the Old Testament. These books were considered to be far more important than any others and were known as the *Torah*.

They also believed that an 'oral law' (advice and laws passed down from generation to generation by word of mouth) was as important as the written Scriptures.

They 'built a hedge about the Law of Moses' to protect it. This meant that the Pharisees made other laws of their own, which people had to obey, to remind them of how important the Torah was.

They believed strongly that all faithful Jews would live again after they had died. This was called 'resurrection'.

Matthew 5:20; Mark 8:15; Luke 11:39.

The Sadducees

The meaning of the name 'Sadducee' is not clear. Some people think that it came from a word meaning 'righteous', whilst others believe that the Sadducees were named after the first High Priest in the Old Testament, who was called Zadok.

The Sadducees were an extremely intelligent group of men, mainly priests, who were rich and owned a great deal of land in Palestine. Some wealthy merchants were also Sadducees. They were not popular with the ordinary people who could not understand their scholarly language. Instead, most people turned to the Pharisees for help. The Sadducees and the Pharisees did not have the same religious beliefs. They were opposing religious groups.

The Sadducees lived by the Law of Moses (the Torah) alone and, unlike the Pharisees, they were not interested at all in any of the old Jewish traditions.

They were great debaters. In fact they spent most of their time talking and debating with each other. They also got on well with the Roman rulers and enjoyed the peace and prosperity that the Roman occupation had brought.

The Sadducees provided most of the important Jewish leaders. The High Priest, for instance, was usually chosen by the Romans from amongst the Sadducees.

They rejected any belief in angels, demons and the resurrection from the dead. They believed that this life was all that mattered.

Matthew 16:1; 22:23–32; Mark 12:18.

24

The High Priest

The Romans chose and appointed the High Priest. He was, therefore, expected to carry out the wishes of the Roman Governor in Palestine. Although this involved the High Priest in politics he was mainly the religious leader of the people. He was based in Jerusalem, where he was seen by the people whilst on duty in the Temple on the Sabbath day and during other religious festivals.

The most sacred task of the High Priest was to enter the holiest part of the Temple, the 'Holy of Holies', once a year. This area was thought to be so holy that no other person was allowed to enter it at any time.

ARK OF THE COVENANT

The High Priest wore the usual white gown of the priest. On top of this he wore a long blue coat. Tassels with bells and pomegranite shapes hung from the bottom of the coat. Over everything the High Priest wore a gold, scarlet and purple cape.

John 18:13,19.

The Sanhedrin

The most important Jewish Council in Palestine was the *Sanhedrin*. Numbering seventy people, the Sanhedrin was mainly made up of Pharisees and Sadducees. It met in the impressive stone chambers underneath the colonnades of Herod's Temple in Jerusalem. Accusations of any crime against Jewish people were brought before the Sanhedrin. Its members sat in a semi-circle and the accused, wearing the clothes of mourning, stood in front of it. Although it had the power to sentence a person to death the Romans had to approve the sentence and carry it out.

Matthew 26:59; John 3:1–21; John 7:50–52.

The Essenes and the Dead Sea Scrolls

One of the most exciting archeological discoveries of all time took place on the shores of the Dead Sea at Qumran in AD 1947. There a Bedouin boy discovered a cave full of old manuscripts. The Dead Sea Scrolls, as they were called, were written by a religious community who lived two thousand years ago. This group of people, known as the Essenes, had withdrawn from normal life and lived in the desert. From the Dead Sea Scrolls we learn that the Essenes lived a communal life. They shared all their possessions, they always ate together, and they baptised each other. They believed that the end of the world would come in their life-time.

These photographs show part of a scroll found in a cave at Qumran, and two of the jars which held scrolls.

The ruins of the Qumran buildings can still be seen today.

The Zealots

The Zealots were the group of Jews who rebelled most strongly against Roman rule. They believed that a true Jew could have no master except God and so the Romans had to be driven out of Palestine. To win this freedom the Zealots were prepared to use violence in the Name of God.

The Zealots found every opportunity they could to demonstrate against the Romans. They refused to pay their taxes and encouraged others to do the same. They kept their weapons ready for an all-out war which they believed could come at any time. Before revolt finally broke out in AD 66, however, there were many smaller rebellions which were ruthlessly put down.

The Romans called the Zealots the 'dagger-men' from the small daggers (*sicarii*) that they carried under their cloaks. In a busy market-place they could plunge these into the backs of unsuspecting Roman soldiers before melting into the crowd.

Luke 6:15.

Masada was the fortress of King Herod. In AD 66 it was taken by the Zealots before they made their last stand against the Romans. In AD 73 the Romans took the fortress but all the Zealots (about one thousand) had committed suicide.

Looking for a Messiah

The Jews believed that one day God would send his blessing upon them, and in that day the people would begin to live in great peace and prosperity. Before that happened God would send a king, descended from the great Jewish King David, who would lead his people into this new era. He was to be the 'Messiah' or Deliverer.

The coming King was known as 'the anointed one'. Amongst the Jews anyone who had been given a special task to do by God was first anointed with oil by a priest. After a series of wars in the second century BC many Jews believed that their Messiah would come soon. They were looking for a warrior who would lead them to victory over the Romans.

When Jesus appeared there were many people who hoped that he was God's chosen Messiah. He may have claimed to be the Messiah, but he was very different from the Messiah that the people were expecting.

Matthew 16:15–17; Mark 1:11; Luke 7:18–23.

Religious festivals

The Jews celebrated three yearly 'foot' festivals. Each of these was linked with a season of the year and the farming calendar (see page 67). They were also closely associated with important events in the history of the Jews when God had shown his goodness to the nation of Israel. These festivals are still celebrated today. They were called 'foot' festivals because as many people as possible travelled to Jerusalem to celebrate each of these Great Festivals. The streets of the city were even more crowded than usual with all the pilgrims

The blowing of the ram's horn (*shofar*) announced the beginning of each new month. It was also the traditional way of ushering in a religious festival – especially the celebrations at the beginning of a New Year.

One of the most important of the Jewish festivals, the Passover (*Pesach*), is held in the Spring. This celebration looks back to the time, hundreds of years earlier, when the Jews left Egypt, where they had lived as slaves, and travelled to their own country, the 'Promised Land'.

Each year at Passover important celebrations take place in the home. Dressed as travellers about to make a journey, members of the family eat a meal together. Each item on the table, amongst them the unleavened (unrisen) bread, reminds them of slavery in Egypt and the journey into freedom which followed. As they eat, the story of these dramatic events is read aloud.

Fifty days after the beginning of the Passover festival came the Harvest festival or the 'Feast of Weeks'. This festival later became known as *Pentecost*. At this very happy festival each Jewish farmer offered the first of that year's crop to God. The gift consisted of two loaves of leavened (risen) bread made from the grain crop which had just been cut.

By doing this the Jews were reminded that their families could be fed only with God's help. Without that help everyone would starve. The first and best of the year's crop, therefore, was offered to God in thankfulness.

At the end of the fruit harvest, the Feast of Tabernacles (booths) provided another opportunity for every Jew to thank God. Pilgrims put up tents or booths all over Jerusalem and then lived in them for eight days. The roofs of the huts were decorated with leaves, fruits and vegetables. This is still done (though in people's own homes), as you can see from this photograph taken of a recent Tabernacles festival.

The festival also remembers the time when God looked after the Jews while they were living in tents (or booths) during their forty years of travelling through the wilderness. They were on their way from Egypt to the 'Promised Land'.

Matthew 26:17–21; Mark 14:1, 2; John 7:1–13.

The Sabbath day

Following the example of God, who rested after spending six days creating the world, every Jewish person also rested on the seventh day of the week (Friday evening-Saturday). This was the Sabbath day and it belonged to God. No work of any kind was to be done.

Food had to be prepared before the day began. Everyone was very busy in the hours before sunset on Friday. The houses were very carefully cleaned from top to bottom.

The first act of the Sabbath day was carried out an hour before sunset. The mother lit a special candle before the family sat down to eat their Sabbath meal. The father then said a blessing over the wine and the bread.

As the first three stars appeared in the sky so the Sabbath day ended. A silver trumpet was blown three times by a priest to mark the Sabbath's end.

31

Jewish people were allowed to take a walk on the Sabbath as long as it was no longer than a 'Sabbath day's journey'. This was about two thousand footsteps – there and back!

At the time of Jesus there was a great debate amongst the Jewish leaders as to what really was 'work'. Some of them would not allow their followers to walk through a corn-field and pick a few grains to eat.

Jewish laws allowed a person to deal with an emergency on the Sabbath. Farmers were allowed, for instance, to pull their animals out of a ditch, and a doctor could attend to a sick person. Opinions differed, however, over exactly what an 'emergency' was.

The Sabbath laws applied to everyone and everything in Palestine. It was a day of rest for animals and servants as well.

Matthew 12:2; Mark 2:27; 3:2.

The synagogues

The Temple built by King Solomon in Jerusalem was the centre of the Jews' religious life. But after it was destroyed in 721 BC the Jewish people had nowhere left to worship God. To make up for this they began to put up simple buildings in which the people could pray, read the Holy Scriptures and be taught. These buildings were called 'synagogues' – the word itself means 'bringing together'.

Soon almost every town and village in Palestine had its own synagogue. There were no priests in the synagogues and no sacrifices took place in them. (Priests were only to be found in Herod's new Temple [see page 36].) In the synagogue an elected committee of ten men chose the man who would teach the congregation. He was known as the 'rabbi'. Any male member of the congregation over the age of thirteen could be asked to read from the sacred scroll or to lead the prayers.

This picture shows the remains of the large synagogue at Capernaum. Below is an artist's impression of the inside of the synagogue as it looked two thousand years ago. Over 60 metres in length, the building was made of white limestone.

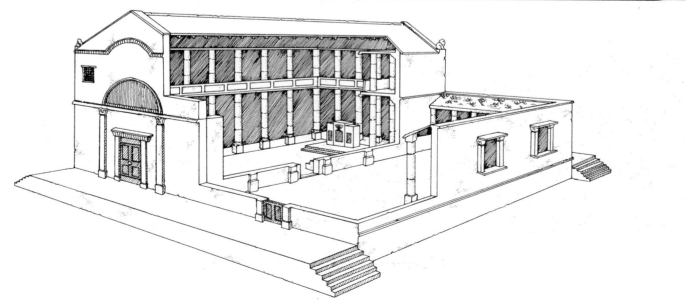

The synagogues were open every day for prayer. They were also open on the Sabbath and for religious festivals. Inside the synagogue was a wooden cupboard called the Ark. It contained the Old Testament scrolls.

The leaders of the synagogue sat on the chief seats in front of the Ark. Before certain prayers could begin ten men had to be present in the synagogue.

The women sat by themselves in a special gallery. At that time they took no active part in the service. (Now, however, women can also be rabbis.) A rabbi usually took the prayers and gave the sermon.

The synagogue teacher was also given the job of punishing those who had done wrong.

The synagogue building was also used as a school. Both adults and children were taught there.

Matthew 12:9; Mark 6:2; Luke 4:15,16.

The Temple in Jerusalem

In 19 BC King Herod began to build his Temple in Jerusalem. It was the third temple to be built there, and the last. Constructed of cream-coloured stone with gold decorations, this Temple was a magnificient sight. Although the Temple building itself took only eighteen months to complete, work continued on the many outbuildings for another eighty years.

There were very strict rules about who was allowed to enter each of the Temple courts. The outer Court of the Gentiles was open to everyone – whether a Jew or not. A notice warned non-Jews (Gentiles) that they would be put to death if they went any further.

Jewish women were only allowed to enter as far as the Court of the Women. In this Court was the Treasury. Here there were thirteen trumpet-shaped offertory boxes in which the people placed their Temple tax. Jewish men could go in as far as the Court of Israel. Only priests could enter the Court of the Priests.

In front of the Temple itself stood a large stone altar. Here the various sacrifices of animals were carried out.

Twelve steps led up to the Temple building. Inside was the Holy Place which had a candle-holder, a table and an altar. A pair of heavy curtains opened into the Holy of Holies. Into this small room only the High Priest could go, once a year.

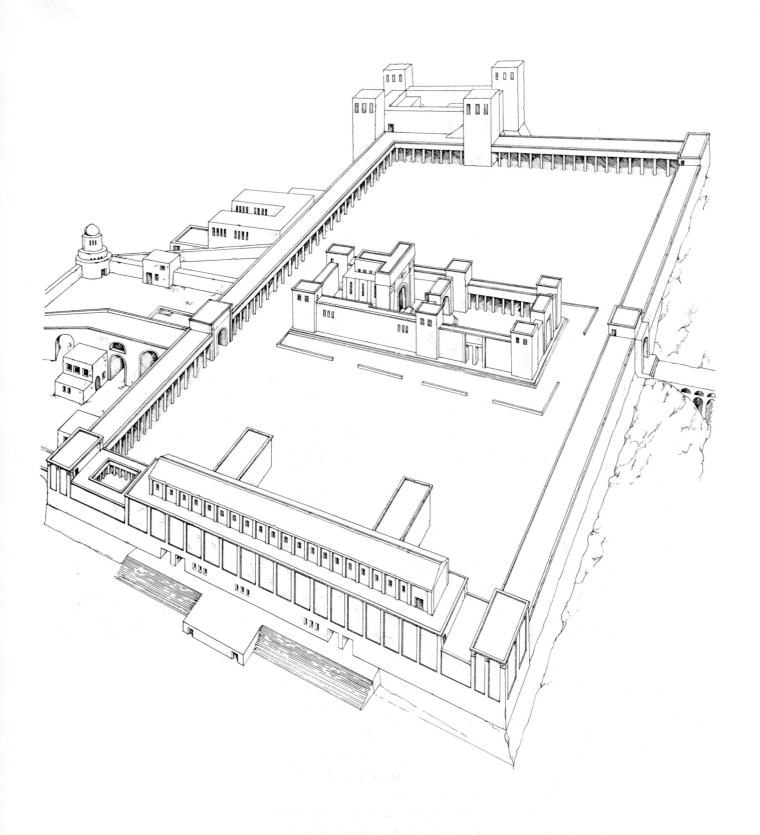

Matthew 4:5–6; 12:6; Mark: 13:1.

Things to do

1. The Dead Sea Scrolls, found in AD 1947, were one of the most important archeological discoveries of all time. Carry out your own research to discover how they came to light after lying hidden for hundreds of years.

2. Imagine that you lived in ancient Palestine in a family with many children. Work out carefully and then describe the preparations that your family would need to make if it was to avoid all forms of work on the Sabbath day.

3. With drawings of your own describe how people celebrated the great festivals of Passover, Tabernacles and Weeks. Find out whether Jews still celebrate all these Feasts today and, if so, how.

4. Below there are some drawings of items mentioned in this unit. Can you identify them?

5. Write a letter to a friend who lives in a small village in Palestine and has never visited the capital city of Jerusalem. Tell her what it is like in the city during the celebrations for the Feast of the Passover, at the time of Jesus.

6. Here are some items taken from this unit. Without looking back try to write two or three sentences about each of them.
    a) The Pharisees. **b)** The Sadducees. **c)** The Essenes. **d)** The synagogue. **e)** The Temple. **f)** The Zealots.

7. Imagine that you are twelve years old and that your parents are taking you to visit the Temple for the first time. Write a letter to your grandmother trying to express something of the excitement and wonder that you feel. It is about AD 12.

8. Try to arrange a visit to a local synagogue so that you can compare the building with that of a synagogue long ago. Are there any great differences? Try to find out the answers to these questions:
   a) When and where were synagogues first built?
   b) What was their main purpose?
   c) Why are no pictures or sculptures allowed in a synagogue?
   d) Are men and women separated inside the building as they were two thousand years ago?
   e) Is the synagogue used for any other purpose than that of worshipping God? If so, what?

9. Copy the following sentences into your books and fill in the missing words from those in the box.

| Sanhedrin | Zealots | The Separated Ones | Scribes |
| Messiah | Holy Scriptures | Holy of Holies | |

   a) The rabbis in the time of Jesus were _____ who taught the _____ _____ to the people.
   b) The word 'Pharisee' means _____ _____ _____.
   c) The most important task of the High Priest was to enter the _____ __ _____ once a year.
   d) The most important Council in Palestine was the _____.
   e) The _____ were the group of Jews most opposed to the Romans being in Palestine.
   f) Jews believed that one day God would send a _____ to deliver them.

10. The three pictures on this page show men and women today celebrating the three great festivals mentioned in this chapter. Can you identify which festival is which?

4. HOME AND FAMILY LIFE

The home and the house

A rich family's house

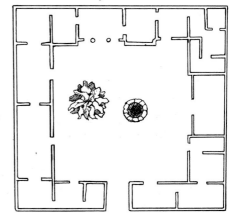

As the above drawing and the plan on the right show, some houses in Palestine were very large. This one had more than twelve rooms. All the rooms led off a central court-yard, and at one end stairs led up to the first floor. The bathrooms and toilets were at the lowest end of the building.

Most Jewish families, however, lived in a one-roomed house. These were usually built out of mud-bricks although people who lived in the highland areas sometimes used stone. Heavy wooden beams were laid across the tops of the walls. Smaller beams were then laid across these beams and over the top layers of brushwood, reeds, mud and grass were placed. The roof-top of the house was flat. Domestic chores could be done there, and the family could relax there at the end of the day.

A poor family's house

Inside the single, badly lit room the floor area was divided into two. The floor itself was usually dirt or clay. Here the family's few sheep or goats lived. The family lived, slept and worked on a raised platform at one end of the room. At night straw mats were laid on the floor and people slept in their working clothes. They covered themselves with their cloaks.

A hole in the earthen floor was made for a fire and the smoke found its way out of the door or the narrow windows. A lamp was kept alight at all times and placed on a special shelf cut into the wall or suspended from the ceiling. Few families could afford much furniture.

The raised platform was also the area where the women usually worked. It was here that they wove at their looms, baked their flat loaves of bread and prepared the food for the family to eat.

Matthew 5:14–16; Mark 2:1–12; Luke 11:5–8.

40

Family life

In the time of Jesus the family at home included not only parents and children but also grandparents, uncles, aunts and cousins as well. Servants were also part of the family. Everyone, from the youngest upwards, had their own work to do.

In every Jewish family the eldest was the supreme authority. His wisdom was expected to guide the family.

The older women taught the younger ones how to run the household. They were also there to help whenever a baby was born to a member of the family.

Children were expected to collect wood for the fire, keep the lamps alight and look after the family's animals.

Men taught their trade to their sons. Jesus's 'father' was a carpenter.

Women had a very busy life. Starting before dawn in the morning they made bread; fetched the water; looked after the children; made clothes and often sold goods in the market-place as well.

The place of women

In Jewish society two thousand years ago women and men had very different roles. The oldest male in the family could, legally, make all of the important decisions without consulting his wife or any other female members of the family.

Children were brought up to obey their parents. When she married, a woman was expected to obey her husband.

In Palestine a man could divorce his wife quite easily. There were no circumstances, however, under which a woman could divorce her husband.

Usually only a man was allowed to own property in Palestine. The one exception was when a father died without having any sons. The property then passed to his eldest daughter.

In Palestine adultery was treated very seriously indeed. It was an old Jewish custom that any women suspected of having been unfaithful to her husband was brought before a priest, who gave her the 'jealousy test'.

Clay and water were mixed in a bowl. The clay made the water very bitter. The woman drank the water and everyone waited to see what would happen. If the water made the woman's stomach swell up she was said to be guilty!

Matthew 5:31,32; 19:3–9; Luke 1:28.

Everyday food

In Palestine the rainfall was unreliable and droughts were common. Pests, such as locusts, could destroy a whole crop in minutes. Each farmer fought a constant battle against the elements to grow enough food to feed the family. Yet when the conditions were favourable, there was a wide choice of food available.

Making bread

Fruit was plentiful and a very important source of food. Sometimes grapes were eaten as fast as they were harvested! Usually, however, they were laid out in the sun, dried and eaten later as raisins.

Many vegetables, like cucumbers, were eaten raw. Others, such as lentils and beans, were boiled in water or cooked in olive oil.

Corn-porridge was made with water, butter and salt. Many different kinds of cakes were made from crushed and malted grain. To sweeten food raisins, figs, dates and especially honey were used.

Meat was a luxury and appeared only on special occasions. When it did it was usually mutton. To cook it the meat was usually boiled although it could be roasted.

Water was not safe to drink, so many families lived on goats' milk. This was kept in skins, like wine. Homemade wine was also very popular, as was fresh grape-juice at harvest time.

People living near to the Sea of Galilee ate fish. They salted them and cooked them over an open fire.

The Jewish food laws

These laws were first laid down when the Jews left Egypt and spent forty years travelling in the wilderness. Food which was approved 'according to the law' was called *kosher*. Jewish people were only allowed to eat meat from animals which chewed the cud and had split hoofs. This meant that eating any part of the pig was strictly forbidden.

    The laws were very strict about the preparation of meat. All of the blood had to be drained out of a carcass before it could be eaten.

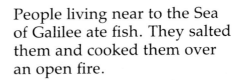

In Palestine midday and evening meals were the most important. In the houses of ordinary people meals were very simple. In the evening a vegetable stew was usually eaten. Meat was added only if a guest was present.

Matthew 26:26; John 2:1–12; 21:12.

A meal in a rich family's house

In a wealthy home the style of eating was very different. Rich Jewish people had adopted Roman-style meals. Nine guests were invited to a dinner-party. They ate their food reclining on couches which were set around three sides of a table. The seating-plan showed the importance of each guest. The closer a person was seated to the host the more important she or he was considered to be.

As the guests arrived their sandals were removed by a servant, who washed their feet.

Three main courses were served to the guests on trays.

Usually pastries and fruit were then served as dessert.

The guests washed their hands several times during the meal, as they ate with their fingers.

Wine was drunk with all courses, but in Jewish homes (unlike Roman) no one was allowed to get drunk.

To finish the evening, dancing and musical entertainment were provided.

Matthew 11:19; Luke 7:36.

Costume and dress

There were strict laws in Palestine against drawing or painting the human figure. As a result we cannot be sure how people dressed two thousand years ago. We can, however, make some intelligent guesses based upon the climate of the country and how people in neighbouring countries dressed at the time.

Poor people's dress

The rich and poor dressed very differently. Most rich people wore a long coat over a long undergarment. The sleeves were wide and the coat was very colourful. Poor people could not afford a coat. There was little difference between the way that men and women dressed.

Rich people's dress

The main item in the wardrobe of a Jewish man was his *colobium*. This was a long and close-fitting tunic. There were openings for the arms and head. Sometimes it was sewn together from two pieces of cloth, sometimes a single piece of linen was used. The *colobium* was often striped. A linen girdle or money belt was tied around the middle.

Matthew 6:19, 25; 22:11–13; Luke 15:22; 16:19.

46

Women

Although women and men wore similar clothes, the women's were longer. The tunic could be hitched up further by tying a girdle around the waist.

Often women tucked up the hem of their tunic to form a bag for carrying things.

Women fetched and carried water jars to and from the local well on their heads, so they steadied the jars by wearing a cloth pad. When they were out of doors women often wore veils over part of their face.

Men

The first thing that a man put on was his loincloth. While he was working he often wore only a loincloth and his head-dress.

Then he put on his *colobium*. This was red, yellow or striped.

A girdle was tied around the waist. Unless the man was rich this was made out of cloth.

In Palestine the sun was so hot that headgear was essential. When working outside, a square of cloth was folded diagonally and a circle of plaited wool used to keep it in place on the head.

Footwear

Palestine was a hot and dusty country. Most people wore sandals on their feet when they were working or travelling.

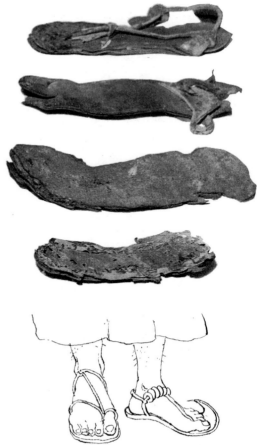

The photographs on the right show sandals found in the caves at Masada (see page 27). These leather sandals were found close to the skeleton of a woman.

Very poor people in Palestine often had to walk barefoot. Children and those mourning the death of a relative also went without sandals.

   The simplest form of sandal was a sole with a leather strap passing between the big and second toes. The wealthy often wore sandals with turned-up toes made out of leather.

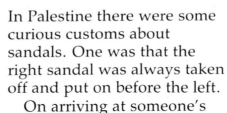

In Palestine there were some curious customs about sandals. One was that the right sandal was always taken off and put on before the left.

   On arriving at someone's house, guests were met outside by the least important servant. The guests' sandals were removed and their feet were washed.

   When property was sold, the seller also gave the buyer a sandal. This showed that the seller no longer had a claim to the property.

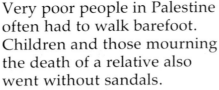

Mark 6:9; Luke 9:5.

Disease and medicine

In Palestine two thousand years ago a combination of poor food, bad water supplies and the hot climate produced frequent outbreaks of cholera, dysentery, typhoid and dropsy. Blindness was widespread, caused by dust particles in the air. Problems at birth were responsible for much deafness and mental disability amongst the people.

Dropsy is caused by liquid in the body's tissue. This brings about some very painful swelling.

Too much acid in the blood affects the kidneys. This causes a great deal of pain in the joints, and lameness. This illness is now known as 'gout'.

Many illnesses were caused by worms in the intestines. These entered the body through contaminated water and were usually fatal, as there was no known cure.

Boils were a severe health problem. A rash and blister-like swellings could cover the whole body. The sufferer died very quickly.

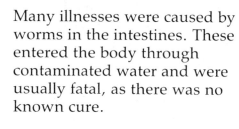

Mental disability was dreaded because the people believed that it was caused by demons. Not only did these demons cause behaviour similar to an epileptic fit, but they were also thought to be responsible for blindness, dumbness and deafness. Attempts were often made to cast the demons out.

Matthew 9:32,33; 12:22; Mark 1:30; Luke 8:28–36.

Blindness was a very common problem in Palestine. Blind people were often to be found by the roadside begging. Leprosy was also a common and much feared disease. Parts of the leprous body lost their feeling and severe ulcers developed.

As leprosy was believed to be highly contagious, lepers were banned from all contact with healthy people. They lived together in a colony on the edge of their town or village.

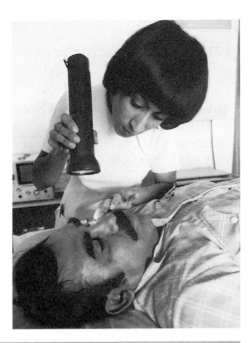

Prevention of disease

Some of the religious laws also helped to keep people as healthy as possible. Disease was almost impossible to cure and so prevention was vital.

All work in Palestine stopped for one day out of seven. This allowed people and animals to rest their bodies. In this way they found enough strength for six days of hard work.

The Jews were not allowed to eat certain kinds of meat. Pork, which was not *kosher*, went bad very quickly and so could cause food poisoning.

Some diseases can be inherited. Jews were not allowed to marry close members of their own family. This would help to prevent such diseases or disorders from being carried on by the children.

The birth of a baby

A mother was helped to give birth by a midwife and the older women in her family. Men were not allowed to be present at the birth. As soon as the baby was born someone went to tell the father.

When the baby was born its umbilical cord was cut and tied. After being washed carefully the child was rubbed all over with salt. This was believed to make the skin firmer and stronger.

The new-born baby was then wrapped from top to bottom in 'swaddling bands'. First a square of cloth was folded around the baby before bandages were wrapped around it tightly. This prevented the baby from moving its arms and legs as this was thought to be harmful to soft, developing bones.

Everyone from the neighbourhood arrived to congratulate the mother on the successful birth. They were very excited indeed if the baby was a boy, because at that time boys were thought to be of more importance than girls. If she could, the mother always breast-fed her baby for many months – even for two or three years. Usually this only stopped when a woman was expecting another baby.

Matthew 1:25; Luke 2:7.

Birth ceremonies

Each new baby was considered to be a gift from God. Soon after it was born special ceremonies were carried out in the Temple. These expressed the thankfulness of the parents to God for the safe delivery of their new baby. They also recognised that the baby had the great privilege of being born into a Jewish family and so was a member of God's Chosen Race.

After a baby boy was born, a woman was said to be 'unclean' for forty days. This length of time was doubled after a girl was born. During this time the women was not allowed to touch any 'holy' object.

To end her 'unclean' state a woman offered a sacrifice of a ram, a pigeon or two doves in the Temple. After doing this she was able to return to normal life.

Each Jewish boy was circumcised by the priest or his father on the eighth day after birth. In this important ceremony the foreskin of the boy's penis was cut off. (This was an old custom which may have started for health reasons.)

Girls were usually given their names at birth and boys when they were circumcised. Names were very important in Jewish families.

A couple's first child was believed to belong to God in a special way. When it was four weeks old the child was 'bought back' from God by paying five silver shekels to the Temple.

A Jewish marriage

FOLDED SILK

FACE POLISHED

HAIR PLAITED

LONG, BROAD VEIL

LONG WHITE DRESS

EMBROIDERY

In Palestine if the two people marrying were young, as they usually were, the parents arranged the wedding and the exchange of money involved. As soon as a price was agreed the groom's father gave a 'bride price' to the girl's family. Her own family also gave a 'dowry' to her. The two people were now betrothed to each other. It was very difficult to break this betrothal arrangement. After some months, or years, the couple then married.

The bride's hair was plaited into an uneven number of strands, and lengths of silk were woven into each plait. Coins were attached to the silk strips. There could be more than a thousand coins in a girl's hair.

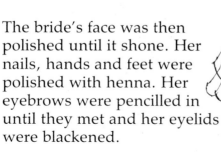

The bride's face was then polished until it shone. Her nails, hands and feet were polished with henna. Her eyebrows were pencilled in until they met and her eyelids were blackened.

Matthew 1:19; 25:1–10; John 2:1–12.

Jewish weddings were very colourful. Before the bridegroom left his house to collect his bride a garland was placed around his neck. In the evening he left with many of his friends and set off for his bride's house. Along the journey, women came out with lighted lamps to meet the bridegroom's procession. It was a great insult if their lamps went out.

Whilst this was happening the bride was being helped to get ready by her bridesmaids.

The bride wore a long white dress embroidered on the ends of the sleeves. Over this she wore a long velvet coat.

The wedding ceremony took place in the bridegroom's house. During the service he lifted her veil.

In an important wedding the Feast that followed could last as long as seven days.

As the guests departed, tired but happy, they wished God's blessing upon the future of the bride and groom.

He tireth easily

54

A Jewish funeral

As soon as someone died, the family, including any servants, began a period of mourning.

When the father of a family died, the eldest son closed the eyelids of the dead man and kissed his lips.

When the family learned of the death they often tore their clothes and put on a rough coat of sackcloth.

Below you can see the funeral of a poor person taking place. There was a mass grave in the Kidron Valley outside the city walls of Jerusalem. This was where the poor people from the area were buried. The bodies of executed criminals were also thrown into the pit which was known as 'Gehenna'.

Matthew 27:7; John 19:40; 20:5; 20:7.

Dressed in its most expensive clothes the body was then wrapped in a white cloth. Coffins were never used. The face was covered with a separate cloth and the hands and feet bandaged.

If the body was buried in a family cave-tomb it was probably necessary to remove other bones first. These were placed in a stone box called an ossuary.

Wealthy families had their own private tombs. These were often hollowed out of the rock and some were very large indeed. The corpses were laid on specially constructed ledges. The entrance to the tomb was covered with a large boulder which rolled along in a groove cut into the ground. The boulder was necessary to prevent wild animals from entering the tomb and taking the bones away.

The photograph shows a modern Jewish burial service.

Mourning

Burial usually took place within eight hours of death and during this time the mourners said special prayers beside the dead person.

As they stood by the body the mourners beat their breasts with the inside of their fists. Sometimes the mourners even pulled out their own hair as a sign of respect for the dead person.

To make mourning as uncomfortable as possible the mourners wore a rough coat of sackcloth.

If the mourners tore their clothes in public this was a great sign of respect.

The mourners often heaped dirt and ashes upon their heads as a mark of respect.

Matthew 13:42; Mark 5:38; Luke 6:25.

Games

If there was no room for children to play games inside their houses they took to the streets or market-place. 'Pretend' games, such as weddings or funerals, were very popular with the children. They also enjoyed playing with such 'modern' toys as whistles, rattles and hoops.

The older children played with knucklebones (or 'jacks') and dice.

Amongst the young men wrestling was very popular. The opponent was thrown by grabbing hold of the belt around the waist.

Hopscotch was a very popular game on the streets. The 'rules' of the game were similar to those of hopscotch today.

Wooden whistles and rattles were very popular with the children.

A favourite 'imitation' game was weddings. The children dressed up as the bride and bridegroom. Other children played the part of guests.

Matthew 11:16–17; 27:35.

Living in a town

In the time of Jesus a town had a wall built around it whilst a village did not. This made the towns much easier to defend against an enemy. The market-place was the centre of town life and was usually to be found just inside the main gate. It was surrounded by open shops selling all kinds of goods.

People came to the market-place to buy and sell from a very wide area round about the town. The poorest arrived there carrying the goods on their backs whilst others weighed down a donkey with them.

In the market, goods were rarely sold for a fixed price. Instead, the seller and buyer tried to agree on a price. Gradually the two parties moved closer and closer together until they met somewhere in the middle! Then they would both be happy with the bargain that they had struck.

A Palestinian town was a very busy place indeed. Along its cobbled streets you would almost certainly have seen these people:

A water-seller with his goatskin bottle on his back. He would bring the water from a well, and have a tray with bowls in front of him. Buyers lifted a brass drinking bowl above their head to pour the water into their mouth.

Baker-boys carrying their flat baskets with barley loaves to sell. These were sold to people who were too busy working to bake their own bread.

A woman buying corn. Having bought the corn the woman then pressed her own name into it with a seal. She then returned later to collect the corn on her way home.

People greeted one another in a very formal way. First there was a long bow, followed by the touching of heart, lips and forehead with the right hand. Friends were kissed three times.

If someone important, such as the High Priest, was coming to visit the town he sent a 'forerunner' ahead of him. It was the forerunner's task to make sure that there was a clear pathway through the crowd for his master.

Women carried their babies in a cradle on their back. The straps of the cradle passed over their head. Women carried their babies like this when they were working, shopping and fetching water.

Matthew 10:11.

Living in a village

Most people in Palestine lived in villages rather than towns. These villages were usually built around a spring of water and were within easy reach of the nearest town.

Apart from farming there were many activities that went on in a typical village. Cheese-making began in May with milk drawn from cows and goats. Poultry farming was a very popular activity and included not only chickens and turkeys but also guinea-fowl, pheasants, peacocks and geese. Bee-hives of various shapes and sizes were also a common sight in Palestine.

Village life was often brightened up by various sports which were very popular with the people. Amongst these were hawking and hunting. During the great religious festivals travelling fairs also arrived in the villages. Puppeteers, acrobats and jugglers were very popular as they made their way from village to village performing for the people.

If an invading army threatened a village the people left it in a hurry and rushed towards the nearest town. Here they found better protection behind the strong walls and alongside the larger population. As soon as the battle was over the people returned to their village and life went back to normal.

Village life was very hard. There was always plenty of work to do:

looking after the animals,   sowing the seed,   baking the bread,

as well as ploughing the fields, spreading the manure, weeding the fields, milking the goat, collecting the eggs, collecting the honey, pruning the vines, collecting the figs, and fetching the water.

Here are three problems that almost all villagers had to face.

Problem 1 – lack of water
Often, in the summer, the local well ran dry and water had to be carried several kilometres. The women did this.

Problem 2 – a marauding army
Soldiers passing through the village would steal food and goods and take captives.

Problem 3 – locusts
Locusts would arrive in a vast swarm and eat all of the vegetation. Within a few minutes a whole year's crop could be destroyed.

Matthew 21:2; Luke 9:6.

Education

Every child's education began at home. Boys were taught by their mothers until they were five or six years of age. At that age they were sent to school. Mothers taught their daughters at home until they left to be married.

The father took a great interest in the religious education of his sons. He taught them about the beliefs and traditions of the Jewish people. He also taught his sons to memorise important passages from the Jewish scriptures.

When they started to work boys were most likely to follow in their father's footsteps. He took great care to pass on all of his skills to them so that they could run the 'family business' when he was too old.

A Jewish girl had many practical lessons to learn from her mother. Before she married she needed to know how to prepare food; how to grind corn and make bread; how to spin, weave and make clothes.

The time soon came for every Jewish boy to go to school. Sometimes the school was held in the open air but it was more likely to be held in the local synagogue or school-house. The teacher sat on a low platform at one end of the synagogue with the children gathered around his feet. Each boy was given a small wooden tablet covered with wax on which to write. The teacher said something to the pupils and they repeated it many times until it was learnt.

Adults also attended classes in the synagogue. Jewish education involved everyone – of all ages.

It was the law that every village and town must contain at least one school.

The older pupils were encouraged to discuss religious matters with the rabbi.

Here is a school in Israel today.

Matthew 6:12–18; 13:55; Mark 9:42–50; Luke 2:46.

Things to do

1. Copy the following sentences into your books and fill in the missing blanks from the words in the box:

   a) Most Palestinian houses were built using _____.

   b) _____ _____ was the most important task of women along with _____ _____ for the family.

   c) In every Jewish family the _____ was the supreme authority.

   d) If any women was suspected of being unfaithful to her husband she took the _____ _____.

   e) People living near to the _____ __ _____ had a plentiful supply of fish to eat.

   f) The main item in the Jewish man's wardrobe was his _____.

2. Imagine that you were responsible for putting together a TV programme to show life in first-century Palestine. Describe which scenes you would include to give as full a picture as possible.

3. Here are drawings of items mentioned in this chapter. Can you identify them?

> eldest   jealousy test
> mud-bricks   grinding corn
> colobium   making clothes
> Sea of Galilee.

4. Here is a picture of the inside of an Eastern house to-day. Compare it with the drawings that you see on page 40. What are the main similarities and differences?

5. What do you think were the main problems of living in Palestine two thousand years ago? How did the people try to overcome these problems? If you had lived then what do you think might have been the most difficult of these problems to live with?

6. With drawings of your own describe the tasks that each member of a Palestinian family was expected to carry out. How do they compare with the work that members of a modern family are expected to do?

7. Here are some words taken from this unit. Explain what they mean in your own words:
   a) *Kosher*.
   b) A locust.
   c) Swaddling.
   d) A dowry.
   e) A loincloth.
   f) Gout.
   g) Mourning.

5. WORK

Farming

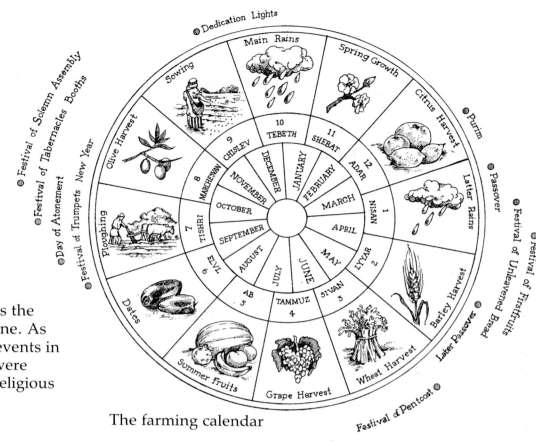

The farming calendar

This diagram illustrates the farming year in Palestine. As you can see the main events in the farming calendar were linked with the great religious festivals.

The farming year

Farmers sowed seed by the 'broadcasting' method. This meant that they carried the seed in a bag and walked along tossing it to left and right. They took little care over where it landed and much of the seed was wasted.

The plough was a simple wooden stake with a handle and a point of iron. Attached to a yoke, the plough was pulled by one or more oxen. Farmers controlled the animals with a long pole.

Everyone in the family helped at harvest time. Flax and barley were harvested in April and wheat a month later. The farmer held the grain in one hand and cut it at the base using a sickle. Then it was gathered into bundles or sheaves.

The grain was then separated from the stalks by threshing. The sheaves were scattered around a hard floor and beaten with sticks or trampled underfoot.

Tithing

To remind them that everything belonged to God, farmers had to give one-tenth of the produce of the land – both fruit and crops – to God. This was called 'tithing'. Farmers also gave one-tenth of their new lambs.

NOT TO BE
PLOUGHED
THIS YEAR

The Jews had been told by God that every field must lie fallow (not be used to grow crops) for one year out of seven. This allowed the soil to recover its goodness and strength.

Matthew 3:11–12; 9:37; 13:1–9; 23:23.

Building

In Palestine there was always a lot of building activity in both town and village. Houses were always needed and city walls had to be extended or strengthened. Wells were dug to obtain a water supply, and cisterns were built to store water.

Building a house

To build a house the bricks had to be made first. A shallow pit was dug and filled with clay and water, then chopped straw was added as a binder. The ingredients were mixed by people walking on them, and the solution was pressed into wooden moulds. The bricks were set out in the sun to dry, then they were cemented into place using a trowel, wooden square and a plumbline. Finally, the walls were put up and wooden beams were laid across the top.

Similar building techniques are still used in many Middle Eastern countries today, as this photograph shows.

Building a water tunnel

Water tunnels were built in the larger towns so that an enemy could not cut off the supply during a siege. Two groups of workers made their way towards each other, shouting at the top of their voices. They met somewhere in the middle!

Matthew 7:24–27; Luke 6:46–48.

Making clothes

The materials most often used for making clothes were sheep's wool, linen (from flax), goat-hair and animal skins. The people loved to wear bright colours and so they dyed the wool. Red and blue seem to have been the favourite colours amongst the men whilst the women preferred blue or green. Amongst the wealthy, purple was very popular. (It was a very expensive dye.)

Fringes and tassles were used to decorate the hems of many garments. In clothes that were made for special occasions a gold thread was often interwoven with the material. Other clothes were most beautifully and elaborately embroidered.

Clothes are still laid out for sale in this Eastern market just as they have been for centuries.

Linen was made from the flax plant. It could be made either coarse and thick or very fine and delicate. It was the wealthy people who wore the most delicate clothes.

Sheep's wool was the most common material for clothes. Many Jews were shepherds and there were plenty of sheep in the country. After the sheep were shorn in the Spring the wool was washed to have its oils removed.

Purple dye was obtained from shell-fish, whilst insects, almonds and pomegranites were also used for dye. The wool was given two washes in the dye before it was ready for spinning and weaving.

Matthew 6:25; 11:8; John 19:23,24.

Spinning and weaving

Spinning

Spinning consisted of twisting and pulling out long threads from bundles of wool. To do this a spindle was turned in one hand whilst the other fed in the wool. The woman fed wool in gently and regularly from an open bowl balanced in her lap or at her side. The bowl had handles inside it which prevented the thread from becoming tangled up.

Although spinning was usually considered to be women's work, as people began to produce more wool to sell in the market so men began to spin as well.

Here a woman is spinning by hand in the traditional way.

Weaving

Weaving was the final process in the production of the finished garment. It seems that almost every Palestinian house had its own loom. Some looms were set upright and loom-weights were attached to the bottom of the warp threads to keep them tight. Other looms were set on the ground and the threads were stretched over a frame. Two sets of threads were fed by the weaver into the loom. The warp threads were stretched lengthwise in the loom whilst the woof threads were passed over and under them.

Weaving was first done by women to meet the needs of their own family. It soon developed, however, into an industry, and men wove as well as women. People still weave by hand in the traditional ways, as these photographs show.

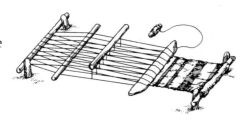

Mark 2:21; Luke 12:27.

The carpenter

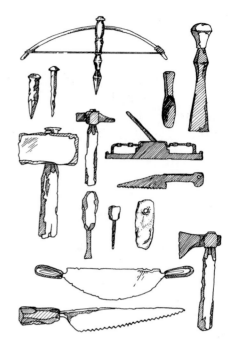

Palestine was short of good native wood so it had to be imported for large building projects from Lebanon and elsewhere. The country was also short of its own gifted carpenters and they were often 'imported' along with the wood. Many carpenters were used by King Herod in building his Temple and most of them came from other countries.

There were carpenters in Palestine, however, who could make all sorts of articles from chariots to household utensils. In ordinary houses any furniture that the family could afford would be made by the local carpenter. In richer people's houses, carpenters made wooden panels, and the doors. In the more elaborate houses, carpenters laid wood upon the basic stone as well as carvings and other forms of decoration.

Here you can see the most common tools which the carpenter used in Palestine. As you will notice many of them are very similar to tools still used today.

Matthew 13:55; Mark 6:3.

The shepherd

Whilst young boys and girls sometimes looked after their family's sheep, larger flocks were the responsibility of a shepherd. He had to make sure that the sheep and goats were safe and well whilst they were grazing away from home. He also moved them from place to place in search of better pasture.

The shepherd's first rule was that the sheep must be protected.

To lose a sheep was a very serious blow to its owner. A sharp lookout always had to be kept for wild beasts, and robbers who often tried to steal the sheep. But the weather was the worst enemy.

To protect his sheep the shepherd lit a fire each night to keep the wild animals away. He counted his sheep whenever he stopped, and built a sheepfold of his own or used one built by someone else. He always kept his ears open for any unusual sound.

The shepherd carried his own food in a knapsack, drank from his own water supply to avoid drinking contaminated water, and lived on curdled milk from the goats in his own flock.

Matthew 25:31–46; John 10:3–6.

Fishing

There was a thriving fishing industry on the shores of the Sea of Galilee. Fourteen different species of fish are known to have been caught there. Whilst most of the fish were eaten by local people or sold in the city of Jerusalem, some were dried or salted, and sold further away.

The life of the Palestinian fishermen was hard and dangerous. A stormy night's fishing might be followed by a day spent in sorting and selling the fish, and mending the nets.

There were four main ways of catching fish.

A light was shone over the side of the boat and the fish were speared. It was difficult to catch many fish in this way.

A bone hook was fitted to a simple line and thrown overboard. The line was then trailed in the water.

A small, circular net called a cast-net was thrown into the water. This then floated on the surface.

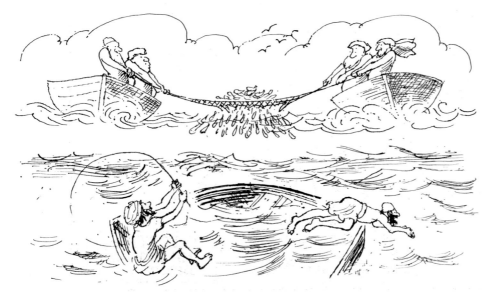

The most effective way of fishing was to stretch a large drag-net between two boats. After the fish swam into the net it was tightened and hauled aboard. Sometimes the catch was so heavy that the net broke.

Storms could blow up very quickly on the Sea of Galilee. Fishermen often lost their tackle or their boats – and sometimes their lives as well.

Matthew 13:47,48; Mark 1:20; Luke 5:5.

Trade

Merchants from Palestine travelled all over the Middle East and beyond, buying and selling goods. Often these traders were away for months, or even years. As they moved around they also carried news of what was happening in the world from one place to another.

When there were no roads between cities traders often had to travel by sea. Sea captains offered a free passage in return for goods.

To trade successfully merchants needed peaceful conditions. Often, however, they found themselves caught up in a war.

Palestine had to import rather more goods than it exported, as the map below shows.

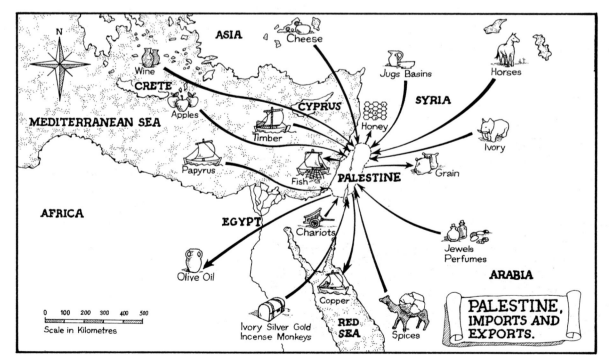

N

ASIA

Cheese

Jugs Basins

Horses

Wine

CRETE

CYPRUS

SYRIA

Apples

Honey

Ivory

MEDITERRANEAN SEA

Timber

Papyrus

Fish

PALESTINE

Grain

AFRICA

EGYPT

Chariots

Jewels
Perfumes

ARABIA

Olive Oil

Copper

Ivory Silver Gold
Incense Monkeys

RED
SEA

Spices

PALESTINE,
IMPORTS AND
EXPORTS.

0   100   200   300   400   500
Scale in Kilometres

Matthew 13:45,46; 18:21–35; John 2:16.

Money and measures

Money

Three different forms of coinage were used in Palestine. Roman money was used all over the Empire. In the provinces Greek money was common, and in the local towns and villages Jewish coins were used.

The coins were minted in gold, silver, copper and bronze.

Coins shown here are one-quarter larger than actual size.

Roman coins:

quadrans

aureus

denarius

ans

Jewish coins:

shekel

lepton

Greek coins:

drachma

stater

Measurements

Short measurements were based upon the human arm. A *cubit* was the distance from the elbow to the fingertip (44.5 cm). The *palm* was the width of the hand at the base of the fingers (7.5 cm). A *span* measured the distance between the thumb and the little finger on the outstretched hand (23 cm).

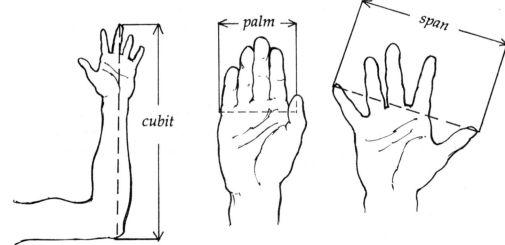

palm

span

cubit

Matthew 6:27; 20:10; Mark 12:15; Luke 15:8.

Travel and transport

Travelling in Palestine was always difficult and dangerous. Although most people travelled short distances on foot there were vehicles that were pushed, pulled or carried by human beings. There were also vehicles that were drawn by animals. However, riding was the most popular way of travelling.

Camels were used for caravan trains whilst horses were used to pull wagons. The main beast of burden was the donkey or mule.

Here is a carving showing passengers travelling in a Roman horse-drawn carriage. Passengers travelled inside the carriage and also on the top.

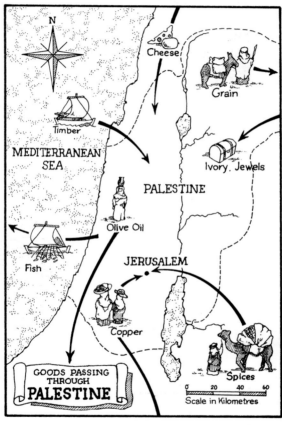

For safety reasons traders often used to travel in convoys. Palestine was criss-crossed by a wide variety of caravan routes and cities grew up at the places where these routes crossed. Goods passed through Palestine on their way to Egypt, Syria and elsewhere.

The people of Palestine were not natural seafarers and rarely used the sea unless it was essential. Their coastline had few natural harbours. The Mediterranean Sea was only safe for ships in the summer months. Between November and March the conditions were very dangerous indeed.

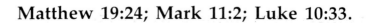

Matthew 19:24; Mark 11:2; Luke 10:33.

Things to do

1. Here are three pictures showing the different stages in the farming year in a Middle Eastern country today. Explain what is happening and how each stage compares with the way it would have been carried out two thousand years ago.

2. Explain, in your own words, what 'tithing' was. Why did the Jewish person pay a tithe? Why do you think that it was an important religious exercise? Find out whether farmers in this country were ever expected to pay tithes and, if so, when the practice ended.

3. Here are some words mentioned in this chapter. Explain what they mean.
   a) Broadcasting.
   b) Threshing.
   c) Dyeing.
   d) Warp and woof.
   e) Cast-net.
   f) Drag-net.

4. Explain, with diagrams of your own, how houses were built in Palestine two thousand years ago.

5. Illustrate and explain some of the different methods people used in Palestine to travel from one part of the country to another.

INDEX